The author with his
long-suffering mother.
Hong Kong, 1973.

Bradley Trevor Greive hails from the untamed island state of Tasmania. During his life, he's worked as an artist, cartoonist, furniture and toy designer, animation director, screenwriter, and paratroop platoon leader.

His previous book, *The Blue Day Book*, also featuring animal photography, is an international bestseller.

BTG currently lives in Sydney.

Also by Bradley Trevor Greive

The Blue Day Book

*Inspiring our community to create a better
future for wildlife and our children*

Bradley Trevor Greive loves animals and proudly supports the Taronga Foundation. To find out how you too can easily make a difference by becoming a Zoo Parent or by making a  donation towards vitally important research and breeding programmes, visit the Taronga Foundation website: www.tarongafoundation.com

Dear Mum

Thank You for Everything

Bradley Trevor Greive

ROBSON BOOKS

This edition first published in Great Britain in 2002 by Robson Books,
64 Brewery Road, London, N7 9NT

A member of **Chrysalis** Books plc

First published by Random House Australia Pty Ltd
20 Alfred Street, Milsons Point
NSW 206
Australia

The author and the publishers have made every reasonable effort to contact all copyright
holders. Any errors that have occurred are inadvertent and anyone who for any reason
has not been contacted is invited to write to the publishers so that a full
acknowledgement may be made in subsequent editions of this work.

British Library Cataloguing in Publication Data
A catalogue record for this title is available from the British Library.

ISBN 1-86105-484-X

Printed by Butler & Tanner, Frome, UK

Acknowledgments

This diminutive yet delightful volume started and finished with Christine Schillig and her team at Andrews McMeel who, once again, have been absolutely superb to work with.

In order to select and procure the amazing animal portraits I was ably assisted by Simone Cater, Jamie Ling, Emma Virgona, Andrew Stephenson, Nicole Glendenning, Pasqualina Grosso, and the incomparable Norma Scott. Special thanks are also due to my creative assistant, Anita Arnold, as well as the perversely generous founder of ABC Interactive, Craig Katz.

Finally I must single out my omniscient agent, Al Zuckerman, at Writers House in New York. If Al had followed his father into the hat business, acted on his secret passion for traditional Irish dance, or become a fur trapper, I would be completely ruined. No question.

All that I am or hope to be I owe to my angel mother.

—Abraham Lincoln

Mum, the other day I was rubbing my belly button
and it really made me stop and think—

what a funny little reminder
of such an important connection,

a connection that reminds me of how I came to be me!

I'm sure it's hard to imagine that I was once small, helpless, and completely dependent on someone else,

but I was.

And that someone else was you, Mum.

You were there to show me my first butterfly

and my first rainbow.

You were there when I took my very first steps
(which looked remarkably similar to my very first hula lesson). 9

You were the first person to make me smile and laugh,
and you were right there to hear my first words—

"Dad-dee!"
(Mum, I am sooo sorry about that.)

It makes me feel wonderful when people say I resemble you, and it's true! We have the same-shaped eyes,

the same ears, the same nose.

And if you look closely, you'll see that
even our toes are similar.

When you think about it, that isn't so surprising—
I will always be a part of you, because you created me.

You sculpted my face with a million tender kisses.

You taught me all the important stuff about our world
and my place in it. I learned everything that matters
from watching you and listening to you.

(And my, my, my, that birds and bees conversation
was a real eye-opener!)

You shared with me all the values that make you so special—
kindness, forgiveness, honesty, persistence, thoughtfulness,
and especially patience!

You also taught me that even the worst day
seems okay with a big mouthful of chocolate.
(Mum, you'd be amazed how often your calming philosophy of
chocolate has carried me through the hard times.)

What I'm saying here, Mum, is that you are the
foundation upon which my character is built.
And I just want to say thank you.

Thank you for always making me feel so
warm, safe, and loved,

for giving me everything I needed (and then some)
to grow up and fulfill my potential,

and for calling me your "perfect little angel"

(despite overwhelming evidence that this
was not actually the case).

Thank you for being my full-time, on-call,
personal chauffeur from day one.

Thank you for your delicious home cooking and for packing so much love and nutrition into my lunch box day after day and year after year.

(And an extra special thank you, Mum, for the
intoxicating smell of freshly baked cakes!)

Thank you for letting a chubby-cheeked two-year-old
run wild among your most precious possessions

and for not saying, "I told you so, I told you so, I told you so," nearly as often as you could have.

Thank you for picking me up whenever
I wanted a cuddle or a better view.

(This probably wasn't too good for your back, Mum.)

Thank you for flying to my rescue every time
you heard me cry out—

"I want my Mum-meeeeeee!!!"

Whenever I got into a bind, you were
always there for me.

You've always known what to say, or what not to say,
to make me feel better.

With your strong, gentle hands, and calm, wise words,
plus lots of warm and loving hugs,

you mended broken toys and broken hearts time
and time again. Thank you, Mum.

Thank you for encouraging me to recognise the
real beauty inside me and to stand tall.

Thank you for telling me I could grow up to be successful
at anything I wanted if only I believed in myself
the way you believed in me.

Mum, I can't tell you how much it meant to know
you were always right beside me, urging me on
to live my dreams.

You gave me enough self-confidence to face all
the challenges of this world with a smile.

But Mum, as wonderful as our relationship has been,
I'm not pretending it was always peaceful and perfect.

I know we got into a flap over things
every now and then

(which rarely ended well for me).

And even though I'm gradually coming to terms
with eating broccoli

and taking that terrible pink cough syrup,

I'm not sure I'll ever get over you making me kiss
your great-aunt smack on the moustache!

But upon reflection, I realise that I'm really the one
who should say, "I'm sorry."

As you may recall, your little bundle of joy
wasn't always a bundle of laughs.

I'm sorry for the times I upset you,

or made you worry about me,

and for all the sleepless nights I caused.

I'm sorry for splashing around in mud puddles after you
dressed me up in my best clothes and new shoes

and for asking, "Are we there yet? Are we there yet?"
every time we went driving.

I'm sorry I tried so hard to sneak out of taking baths

and for sulking when you made me go to school
or wouldn't let me get a Mickey Mouse tattoo
or get my tongue pierced. . . .

I'm truly sorry for the times I was downright nasty
and difficult (especially in nice restaurants)!

And I do feel bad about all the 5 A.M. in-your-face
wake-up calls on my birthdays, Christmas morning,
and all those times I was too excited to sleep.

I'm really sorry I didn't give you more time to yourself.
Even just a few more quiet moments to think, to dream.

I realise now what a tremendous sacrifice you made for me.
I know my playtime took precedence over your rest time,

my meal times took precedence over your meal times,

and my potty training took precedence
over absolutely everything.

Then every time you tried to relax,
I'd burst into the room with outrageous demands, like:

"Mum, I'm starving!"

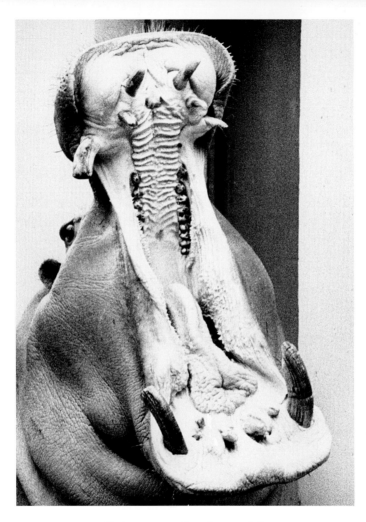

"Mummy, I'm bored."

"Mummy, I can't find my pet chicken anywhere.
I need you to wake up and help me find it right now!"

Frankly, I'd be lost without you, Mum, and I only wish
I had more than one lifetime to repay the
incredible debt I owe you.

You have shown me a world filled with love and wonder,

you have put me on the path to a rich and rewarding life,

and you have made me happier than
you could possibly imagine.

I want the whole world to know:
MY MUM IS THE GREATEST MUM IN THE UNIVERSE!

Because you are.
Thank you, Mum. Thank you for everything.